Self-Care Journal

FOR YOUNG ADULTS

PROMPTS AND PRACTICES TO CREATE HEALTHY HABITS AND **NURTURE YOU**

BRIANA HOLLIS,
LSW

ROCKRIDGE PRESS

For general information on our other products and services or to obtain technical support, please contact our Customer Care Department within the United States at (866) 744-2665, or outside the United States at (510) 253-0500.

Rockridge Press publishes its books in a variety of electronic and print formats. Some content that appears in print may not be available in electronic books, and vice versa.

TRADEMARKS: Rockridge Press and the Rockridge Press logo are trademarks or registered trademarks of Callisto Media Inc. and/or its affiliates, in the United States and other countries, and may not be used without written permission. All other trademarks are the property of their respective owners. Rockridge Press is not associated with any product or vendor mentioned in this book.

Interior and Cover Designer: Lisa Schreiber
Art Producer: Hannah Dickerson
Editor: Eliza Kirby
Production Editor: Rachel Taenzler
Production Manager: Jose Olivera
Illustrations © Alexandr Bakanov/Creative Market, pp. IV, VIII, 34, 70, 104; All other illustrations used under license from iStock.com

ISBN: Print 978-1-64876-960-3

R0

This journal belongs to:

_____

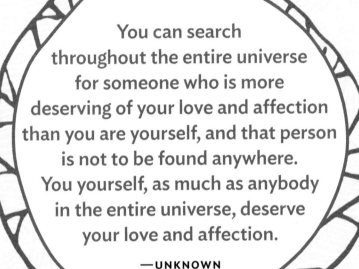

You can search
throughout the entire universe
for someone who is more
deserving of your love and affection
than you are yourself, and that person
is not to be found anywhere.
You yourself, as much as anybody
in the entire universe, deserve
your love and affection.

—UNKNOWN

Contents

Introduction

Welcome! I'm so glad that you decided to learn about practicing self-care. No matter who you are, I promise you can find some nuggets of wisdom in this book.

My name is Briana, and I'm a licensed social worker and life coach. For nearly a decade, I've been helping people of all ages, but especially young people, with their mental health.

I first started focusing on self-care when I felt burned out myself. I was working full-time and in graduate school. I was helping so many people that I forgot to take care of myself. I was tired and frustrated, and I sometimes had trouble sleeping.

After months of feeling like this, I had to do something. I took a semester off from school and found my own life coach. She helped me focus on my self-care. With this book, I hope to do the same for you.

What Is Self-Care?

Self-care is a way for you to take an **active and intentional** role in your happiness and well-being. It looks different for everyone. For example, one of my favorite ways to practice self-care is reading. I love curling up under a blanket with a book. But if you don't like reading, doing it for self-care could feel like the worst thing in the world. An important part of self-care is finding a practice that works for you.

You might be wondering why you should practice self-care. Self-care is vital for everyone, especially young adults.

Did you know that, according to a 2018 report by the American Psychological Association, 91 percent of young adults have experienced at least one physical or emotional symptom of stress? Stress can come from anywhere: school, work, relationships, social media, or new responsibilities. Self-care helps you remain centered in times of stress, crisis, or uncertainty.

It is important to try to practice a little bit of self-care every day. It might feel like a chore at first. But this book is here to help you create a self-care practice that can fit seamlessly into your busy life.

How to Use This Book

This book is a space for you to reflect, identify what self-care means to you, and create positive habits. Together, these activities can help you relieve stress and anxiety and bring calm to your life.

The exercises and journal prompts in this book will challenge you to check in with yourself and deepen your self-awareness. I don't expect you to try them all right away, so take your time.

You'll find that you like some suggestions or prompts more than others. You may find some you want to return to and some that don't work for you at all. That is totally okay! Self-care is personal.

While this book can help you create a self-care practice, it isn't a replacement for therapy, medication, or medical treatment. If you believe that you need any of these things, I strongly encourage you to seek them out. There is no shame in asking for help. I've done it numerous times. Some of the exercises or prompts in this book may be triggering for you. In the Resources in the back of this book, I've included crisis intervention services you can contact any time, day or night, if you need someone to talk to.

Caring for yourself opens you up to many new opportunities for growth. This book is the start, but I know you'll take it even further. You're ready for this!

The creation of a
thousand forests
is in one acorn.

—RALPH WALDO
EMERSON

Small Choices

When you hear the word "self-care," what do you think of? I'm going to take a guess and say that it probably brings up images of people lounging in bathtubs or getting facials at a spa. While those activities can be self-care (and are for many people), they are not the only kind of self-care that matters.

One of the myths that I would like to dispel about self-care is that it has to be big, expensive, and focused on your physical body. Self-care can absolutely be the small and sometimes (seemingly) inconsequential moments, and choices, of everyday life.

One simple self-care technique is called "grounding." Grounding helps you focus on the present instead of unwanted thoughts or feelings. There are many ways to practice grounding, such as counting items or even holding a piece of ice. My favorite way to ground myself is by using the five senses. To practice this technique, follow these steps:

Name five things you can see

Name four things you can touch

Name three things you can hear

Name two things you can smell (or two of your favorite scents)

Name one thing you can taste (or one thing that you like to taste)

You can do this anytime you're feeling stressed or upset, no matter where you are. Try it the next time you need a moment to calm yourself.

Today, I will practice self-care by _____

Mood Tracker

We all know about New Year's resolutions, but rarely do we make resolutions at any other time of the year. A resolution is just a commitment to do something (or not do something), and you don't have to wait until January 1 to make one. Let's make a firm commitment to self-care for tomorrow. What's your self-care resolution for tomorrow going to be?

_____

_____

_____

_____

_____

_____

_____

_____

_____

_____

_____

Today, I will practice self-care by _____

Mood Tracker   😄   🙂   😐   😲   😧   😟   😖   ☹️

To start thinking about what your self-care plan could look like, try writing about what a perfect day would look like for you. What types of things are you doing? What environment are you in? Who are you sharing the day with? Do your best to visualize it, and write down even the small details.

Today, I will practice self-care by _____

_____

Mood Tracker 😄 🙂 😐 😮 😟 🙁 😕 😣

We all have simple pleasures that we enjoy. One of my simple pleasures is being outside at night, especially in the fall and winter. I love how quiet it is and the crisp smell of the air. What is a simple pleasure that you enjoy? Write about it in detail.

Today, I will practice self-care by _____

Mood Tracker

Another one of my favorite ways to practice self-care is cooking. My favorite recipes are the simple ones that I can throw together by the time an episode of my favorite TV show is over. So, let's make a recipe for self-care! Feel free to keep your recipe super simple. Here's an example:

> *10 minutes of music*
> *1 text to a friend*
> *1 cuddle session with a pet*
> *2 pieces of chocolate*
> *Repeat as needed*

What's your recipe? You can use it whenever you feel the need. Don't forget that you can change it up, too.

Right before you start getting overwhelmed or anxious, you may feel sensations coming up in your body. When I get anxious, I feel it in my stomach: usually the classic "butterflies," but sometimes something more extreme, like a huge, growing lump in my abdomen. The next time you're getting upset, notice where you feel it in your body. Is it in your head, like the beginning of a headache? Is it in your hands? Do they get sweaty? Just notice the sensations. They aren't good or bad. They just are.

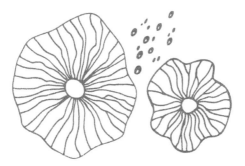

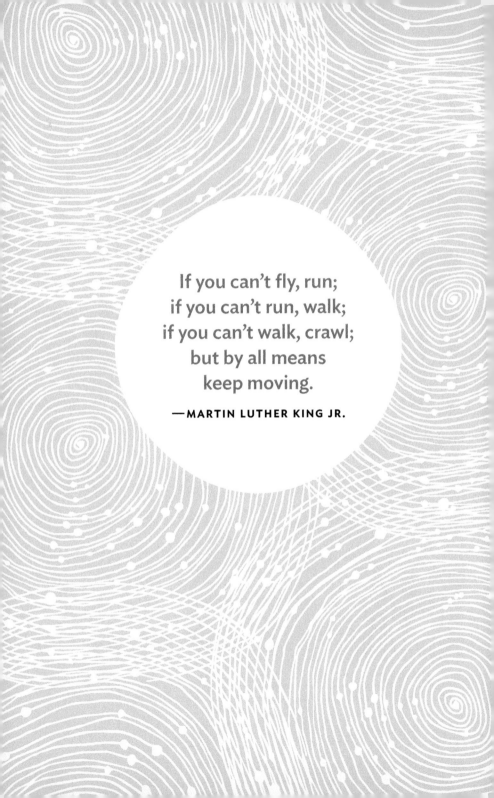

If you can't fly, run;
if you can't run, walk;
if you can't walk, crawl;
but by all means
keep moving.

—MARTIN LUTHER KING JR.

Today, I will practice self-care by _____

Mood Tracker 😄 🙂 😐 😮 😢 🙁 ☹️ 😞

Finding small amounts of happiness can be challenging—not because they aren't there, but because we don't always remember them. Do you remember that time when you saw the most incredible sunset or heard a joke that made you laugh so hard you nearly peed yourself? You might, but then again you might not. Use the space below to record some of the little moments of happiness that you experienced this week. Any time you are feeling down, come back to this page and read about all of the little things that made you happy.

Today, I will practice self-care by _____

Mood Tracker 😄 😊 😐 😮 😢 😕 ☹ ☹

You're probably familiar with experiments from years of science classes. One of the reasons to perform an experiment is to learn something new. For this self-care experiment, try out a new self-care technique or tool, like the grounding technique on page 2, and write down your findings. What did you learn? Did anything surprise you?

Today, I will practice self-care by _____

| Mood Tracker | 😁 ☺️ 😐 😯 😣 🙁 ☹️ 😞 |

Laughter is definitely a form of self-care. What are some things that make you laugh? It could be people, pets, movies, comedians, or anything else you can think of. List these things below. When you feel like you need a laugh, come back to this page and pick one from the list.

_____

_____

_____

_____

_____

_____

_____

_____

_____

_____

_____

_____

_____

Today, I will practice self-care by _____

Mood Tracker   😄 🙂 😐 😯 😟 😕 🙁 ☹️

We all need support sometimes, and there are people out there who want to help. Asking for help is a form of self-care and self-advocacy. And when we ask for help once, it gives us the courage to do it again. What is a small thing that you need help with? This could be as minor as needing guidance with homework. Who could help you with this?

Today, I will practice self-care by _____

Mood Tracker 😄 🙂 😐 😯 😢 🙁 😞 😣

The smallest things can bring us comfort when we're feeling anxious or upset. When I'm upset, just wrapping myself in a blanket can help me feel better. What are the small things that usually bring you comfort?

An easy way to practice self-care is by focusing on your breathing. When you're feeling overwhelmed or anxious, you may notice that your breathing changes. It might get rapid or shallow. You may feel like you're not getting enough air. "Box breathing" or "square breathing" is a technique that can help you regain a steady rhythm. Here's how to do it:

Breathe in (through your nose) for four seconds

Hold for four seconds

Breathe out (through your mouth) for four seconds

Hold for four seconds

Repeat as needed

You might find this exercise a little hard to do at first. That's okay! Do what feels right for your body.

There is a powerful
force unleashed when
young people resolve
to make a change.

—JANE GOODALL

Today, I will practice self-care by

Mood Tracker 😄 🙂 😐 😮 😢 😕 😔 ☹️

It is a myth that self-care has to involve large actions. Today, I'd like you to think of something that is bothering you or something you feel is holding you back from being your happiest self. You don't need to make an entire action plan to conquer it. However, what would make this situation 5 percent better or 5 percent easier to deal with?

Today, I will practice self-care by _____

Mood Tracker 😃 🙂 😐 😯 😢 🙁 ☹️ 😞

Let's try to come up with a self-care mission statement. A mission statement is usually a summary of an organization's values and goals. But people can have mission statements, too. Think about what your values and goals are now that you know a little bit more about self-care.

_____

_____

_____

_____

_____

_____

_____

_____

_____

_____

_____

_____

_____

_____

_____

_____

Today, I will practice self-care by _____

_____

Mood Tracker   🙂 🙂 😐 😮 😢 🙁 😔 ☹️

How we start the day can really affect how the rest of the day goes. How do you start your day? Write down all of the steps that you take to get ready in the morning. How many of those steps include actions that you would consider self-care? How can you add self-care to your morning routine?

Today, I will practice self-care by

You're probably familiar with the mottos or slogans of your favorite brands. These are short statements that tell you something meaningful or memorable. You're in the middle of creating your own brand of self-care. So, what's your self-care motto? Repeat it to yourself whenever you need a reminder of what self-care means to you, and feel free to come up with multiple mottos if you like.

It may seem like you have no time for self-care. You're in school or working, taking care of family members, and lots more. But today, carve out 10 minutes to focus on your self-care. This could be in the morning before you start your day, right before bed, or any time in between. If you feel comfortable, you can even let others know that you'll be taking this time for yourself so that they can give you a bit of space.

Today, I will practice self-care by _____

Mood Tracker   😃 🙂 😐 😮 😟 🙁 ☹️ 😞

Sometimes you may find yourself feeling stuck and focused on one thing that is causing you anxiety or frustration. What's the one thing that you're feeling stuck on today? Was there a time in the past when you were stuck on something similar? What was something small that helped you get unstuck then?

Like what
you do; then you
will do your best.

—KATHERINE JOHNSON

Today, I will practice self-care by _____

Mood Tracker   😃 🙂 😐 😯 😢 🙁 ☹️ 😔

Listening to music is a great form of self-care. It can help us express how we feel when we don't have the words. Write a list of your favorite songs here. Once you're done, go ahead and listen to them or make them into a playlist.

_____

_____

_____

_____

_____

_____

_____

_____

_____

_____

_____

_____

_____

_____

Today, I will practice self-care by

Mood Tracker

Everyone has tough days. Even the happiest person will tell you that they have bad days. But what makes a day hard is different for everyone. It could be not getting enough sleep or needing to do a task you don't enjoy. What makes a day challenging for you?

Today, I will practice self-care by _____

Mood Tracker ☺ ☺ ☺ ☺ ☺ ☺ ☺ ☺

There is something that you can look forward to in nearly every day. But you may have to think a little bit to figure out what that thing is. Take a few minutes to write about what you're looking forward to today or tomorrow.

Creating a self-care box is a small but helpful step that you can take toward a better self-care practice. A self-care box is just a box of the things that you use when you're practicing self-care. Gather together some items you might want to include, such as snacks, your favorite book, or a comforting item like a stuffed animal. When you need a bit of self-care, bring out your box.

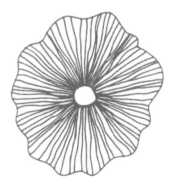

Today, I will practice self-care by

| *Mood Tracker* | | | | | | | | |

Sometimes self-care means removing the little annoyances from our lives. I'm sure you can think of plenty of minor annoyances that, while small, can leave you in a bad mood. Take a few minutes to think about the little things in your life that annoy you and write them down here. Which minor problems can you do something about?

Today, I will practice self-care by _____

Mood Tracker   😁 🙂 😐 😮 😢 🙁 😞 😠

Between homework, work, cleaning, and all of our other commitments, we all wish we could have a couple of hours more each day to get everything done. However, we rarely think about wanting more hours so that we can practice self-care. If you could add just one more hour to your day, how would you use that hour to practice self-care?

Today, I will practice self-care by _____

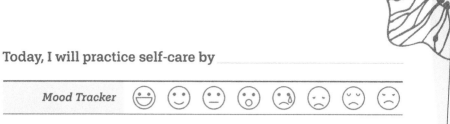

Mood Tracker

The smallest things can provide us with hope that tomorrow will be better. Write down something that inspired you today. It could be something that you did, something that happened to you, or even something that you learned about online.

Today, I will practice self-care by _____

Mood Tracker ☺ ☺ ☺ ☺ ☺ ☺ ☺ ☺

How you end your day can be just as important as how you start it. The close of the day can be a time to reflect on how the day went and what you'd like to do tomorrow. How do you end your day? What steps do you take to slow down your mind and body before heading to bed? How does self-care fit into your nightly routine? Is there anything that you would like to add to your routine?

Today, I will practice self-care by _____

Mood Tracker 😄 🙂 😐 😮 😟 🙁 ☹️ 😦

Superheroes and superhero movies are incredibly popular right now. Having a superpower would be pretty great! If you could have any superpower, how would you use it for self-care?

_____

_____

_____

_____

_____

_____

_____

_____

_____

_____

_____

_____

_____

_____

_____

Today, I will practice self-care by _____

Mood Tracker   😄 🙂 😐 😮 😟 🙁 😕 😞

Let's get back to the basics. Self-care is essentially taking care of yourself so that you are happy and contributing to your well-being. What self-care practices are essential for your happiness or overall well-being? For example, getting enough sleep or rest is necessary to keep your body healthy.

_____

_____

_____

_____

_____

_____

_____

_____

_____

_____

_____

_____

_____

_____

Today, I will practice self-care by

Mood Tracker 😀 🙂 😐 😮 😖 🙁 ☹️ 😞

In previous prompts and exercises, I've asked you to come up with simple things you can do for your self-care. Now I want you to think about the significant effects all of these simple things together can have on your life. Where do you see yourself in two years after adding some simple self-care practices to your daily routine?

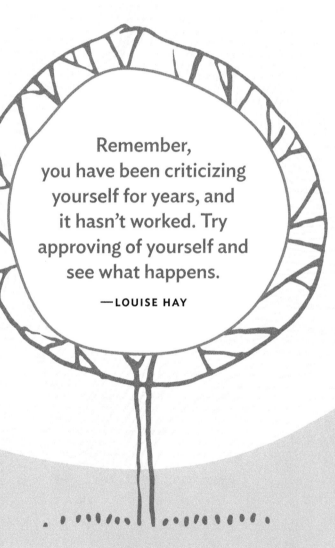

Remember,
you have been criticizing
yourself for years, and
it hasn't worked. Try
approving of yourself and
see what happens.

—LOUISE HAY

Body Kindness

Now that we've tackled the small choices we make each day, we can feel empowered to conquer larger aspects of our lives.

This section of the journal is all about "body kindness," or how you can be kind to your body so that it can support you in your well-being.

Body kindness looks different for everyone. This section will help you explore what it means to you.

Today, I will practice self-care by _____

Mood Tracker 😄 🙂 😐 😮 😢 😣 😔 🙁

One of the easiest ways to control your environment is by determining what you want in it. Take a look around your room, and choose what you like and don't like. Make a list of things you may want to get rid of and things you want to keep.

TO KEEP	TO GET RID OF

Today, I will practice self-care by _____

Mood Tracker 😄 🙂 😐 😮 😟 🙁 😔 😣

Our senses can provide us with many small pleasures that we often don't notice because we're used to them. Today, focus on your five senses. What is something about each sense that you're grateful for? An example: I'm grateful for my sense of smell because it lets me smell freshly baked brownies.

_____

_____

_____

_____

_____

_____

_____

_____

_____

_____

_____

_____

_____

Today, I will practice self-care by _____

Mood Tracker   😀   🙂   😐   😮   😢   ☹️   😖   😣

We all have different definitions of what it means to be healthy. There is no "one size fits all" definition because we all have different needs, bodies, and minds. What does being healthy mean to you? Is it how you look? How you feel? Or something else?

_____

_____

_____

_____

_____

_____

_____

_____

_____

_____

_____

_____

_____

Did you know that having a lot of stuff around you can make you feel overwhelmed? The same can happen when things aren't in their right "spot." Take a look around your room. Do you have items you don't need or want anymore? Are there things that aren't where they should be? For an hour, try your best to declutter your room. You can donate or sell the things that you no longer want or need. Don't forget the things you listed on page 36!

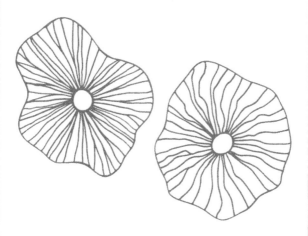

Today, I will practice self-care by _____

Mood Tracker   😄 🙂 😐 😮 😢 😕 🙁 ☹️

Sometimes being kind to your body is about making a different choice than you would typically make. These choices could be about what you eat, what you wear, or where you go. What is one small choice you can make today to be kinder to your body?

Today, I will practice self-care by _____

_____

| *Mood Tracker* | 😁 | 🙂 | 😐 | 😮 | 😟 | 🙁 | ☹️ | 😣 |

Your name is a unique part of who you are. Let's use it to build up
some body kindness. Write out your name vertically, and for each
letter, come up with one positive word starting with that letter to
describe your body. For example, S = Strong.

_____

_____

_____

_____

_____

_____

_____

_____

_____

_____

_____

_____

_____

_____

You will never
gain anyone's approval
by begging for it. When you
stand confident in your own
worth, respect follows.

—MANDY HALE

Today, I will practice self-care by _____

_____

Mood Tracker 😀 🙂 😐 😯 😢 🙁 😔 😖

Sleep and rest are essential to keeping our bodies functioning. But finding enough time to rest between all of our responsibilities can be challenging. Take a few minutes to think about your current sleeping habits. How long do you sleep every night? Do you feel rested when you wake up? Is there anything that you feel needs to change?

"Body movement" involves moving your body in any way that feels good to you (in contrast to "exercise," which can have more negative connotations). You do not need to go to a gym or have expensive equipment to engage in body movement. For this self-care practice, pick a physical activity that you'd like to do. This could be yoga, playing basketball, taking a walk, or even playing tag with your younger siblings. After you're done, notice how your body and mind have changed (for better or worse). You won't love every potential form of body movement, but eventually you'll find one that you do like.

Today, I will practice self-care by _____

Mood Tracker   ☺ ☺ ☺ ☺ ☺ ☹ ☹ ☹

The way you look is only a small part of who you are. But this one element can be amplified out of proportion because it is often the first thing that we show to the world. List at least five positive affirmations about your body and appearance. It may take a while, but keep going until you have at least five.

Today, I will practice self-care by _____

Mood Tracker   😄 🙂 😐 😮 😢 😕 ☹️ 😣

You might be surprised to hear this, but sleeping is not the only way that you can rest. And honestly, sleeping can be challenging for some people. Sometimes rest might look like closing your eyes while you listen to music. Other times it could be standing against a wall and watching the world go by. What are some ways you can rest even if you can't sleep right now?

_____

_____

_____

_____

_____

_____

_____

_____

_____

_____

_____

_____

_____

Today, I will practice self-care by _____

Mood Tracker 😄 🙂 😐 😯 🙁 😕 ☹️ 😣

Being healthy is important. It also doesn't look the same for everyone. The way you think about your health may be different from the way other people in your life do, especially if you have a disability or a chronic illness. What are you currently doing to help maintain or better your physical health?

_____

_____

_____

_____

_____

_____

_____

_____

_____

_____

_____

_____

_____

_____

_____

_____

Today, I will practice self-care by _____

Mood Tracker 😄 🙂 😐 😮 😟 😔 😫 ☹️

Being kind to our bodies means knowing the limits of what they can do. There may be times when you want to stay up all night or save an hour by skipping lunch. But your body needs rest and food to feel its best. How do you push the limits of your body, and what can you do better?

_____

_____

_____

_____

_____

_____

_____

_____

_____

_____

_____

_____

_____

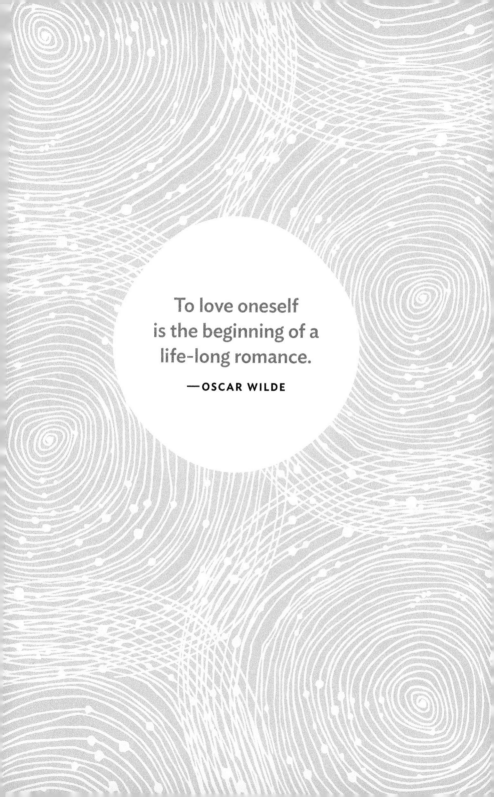

To love oneself
is the beginning of a
life-long romance.

—OSCAR WILDE

One of the best ways to figure out how a particular food or drink affects our bodies is by eating or drinking mindfully. No food or drink is bad, just different in how our bodies react to it. The next time you eat something or take a drink, notice how it feels on your tongue or how it moves down your throat. Notice how it tastes and how it makes the rest of your body feel. Does it leave you energized? Tired? Try this with different foods. You'll begin to learn what foods make you feel your best.

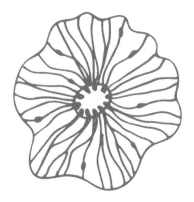

Today, I will practice self-care by _____

Mood Tracker   😃 🙂 😐 😮 😟 🙁 ☹️ 😞

You probably say a lot of things to yourself about your body, both positive and negative. But what about the opposite? If your body could talk to you, what do you think it would say?

Today, I will practice self-care by _____

A vital part of being kind to our bodies is making sure we take care of ourselves when we experience physical pain. Pain feels different for everyone, and what works for you may not work for someone else. What can you do for yourself when you're feeling physical pain?

_____

_____

_____

_____

_____

_____

_____

_____

_____

_____

_____

_____

_____

_____

Today, I will practice self-care by _____

_____

Mood Tracker 😀 🙂 😐 😮 😣 🙁 😖 ☹️

Our environment can have a considerable impact on how we feel about ourselves. Think about where you currently live. This could be as broad as your city, state, or country, or as local as your neighborhood. What do you like about it? What do you dislike about it?

_____

_____

_____

_____

_____

_____

_____

_____

_____

_____

_____

_____

Today, I will practice self-care by _____

Mood Tracker 😄 🙂 😐 😲 😓 🙁 😔 ☹️

The way we view our bodies often is framed by the way society
believes bodies "should" look. When we don't fit this particular fram-
ing, it can cause distress. When society tells you that you "should"
look a certain way, what will you tell society instead?

Today, I will practice self-care by _____

Mood Tracker   😄 🙂 😐 😮 😟 🙁 ☹️ 😣

Songs can make us feel more powerful and confident. This confidence can even extend to how we feel about our bodies. Write down a list of songs that make you feel confident about your body. When you lack confidence, listen to these songs to inspire yourself.

If your compassion
does not include yourself,
it is incomplete.

—JACK KORNFIELD

Today, I will practice self-care by _____

Mood Tracker 😀 🙂 😐 😮 😢 🙁 ☹️ 😣

One of the ways that we moved our bodies when we were younger was through playing. Think about all the games you might have played when you were a child, like Simon Says, tag, or hopscotch. How did those activities help you move your body? Would those types of body movements still feel fun today?

Today, I will practice self-care by _____

Mood Tracker 😃 🙂 😐 😮 😰 🙁 ☹️ 😣

There's a saying that goes, "Home is where the heart is." The environment where you currently live may not feel like home. So, where do you feel most at home? What makes you feel that way about this place?

_____

_____

_____

_____

_____

_____

_____

_____

_____

_____

_____

_____

_____

_____

Today, I will practice self-care by

While self-care isn't always about pampering yourself, sometimes it is. Pampering doesn't have to be super luxurious; little treats count, too. What are some small ways that you can pamper yourself? How about taking a nap in the middle of the day or eating an extra piece of your favorite dessert?

It can be hard to find a moment for yourself when you're being interrupted with notifications from your phone, tablet, or computer all day. Today, turn these off. You can disable notifications for many apps and limit the time you spend on your devices; often, it's as simple as going into the settings for each app and device. Assess how you feel at the end of the day.

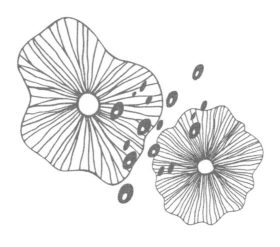

Today, I will practice self-care by _____

Mood Tracker 😄 🙂 😐 😮 😧 🙁 ☹️ 😞

In some ways, our bodies can make us feel disappointed. And that's okay! You do not have to love your body 24/7 to be kind to it. Write a list of some of the disappointments that you may be feeling about your body today. Even though you're disappointed, how can you still be kind to yourself?

Today, I will practice self-care by _____

Mood Tracker   😁 🙂 😐 😮 😢 😟 😞 🙁

Our bodies grow and change year to year and even week to week. There's probably something your body once couldn't do that it can do now. Show your body some appreciation today and list all the things it can do now that it couldn't do a year ago.

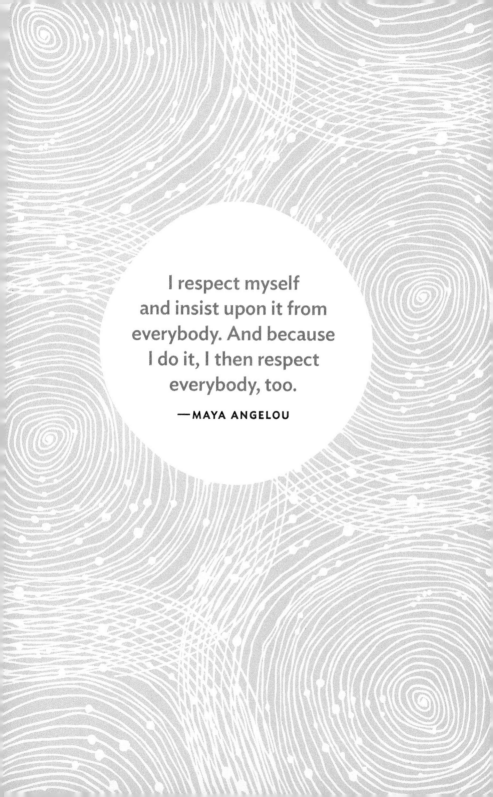

I respect myself
and insist upon it from
everybody. And because
I do it, I then respect
everybody, too.

—MAYA ANGELOU

Today, I will practice self-care by _____

Mood Tracker   😃 🙂 😐 😮 😢 😟 ☹️ 😣

We all have items that, no matter how long we've had them, we can't seem to get rid of. These could be things with sentimental value or things we think could be useful in the future. What's one item that you can't throw out? What are all of the reasons you don't want to part with it? If you need to, refer back to the list of things you wanted to keep and get rid of on page 36.

_____

_____

_____

_____

_____

_____

_____

_____

_____

_____

_____

_____

_____

Today, I will practice self-care by _____

| Mood Tracker | 😀 | 🙂 | 😐 | 😮 | 😢 | 😞 | 😔 | 🙁 |

Over the past few years, many celebrities have spoken out about being kind to our bodies. Who do you admire for their body kindness or body confidence? What makes them admirable?

_____

_____

_____

_____

_____

_____

_____

_____

_____

_____

_____

_____

_____

_____

_____

_____

We all have things in our wardrobes that make us feel great when we wear them. This could be because they fit well, they're our favorite color, or they help us express ourselves. Take a look in your closet (or that chair that you keep your clothes on) and find one thing that makes you feel good. Wear it for the rest of the day and notice how you feel.

Today, I will practice self-care by _____

Mood Tracker   😃 ☺️ 😐 😮 😢 😕 😟 😣

Everyone deserves to live in an environment in which they can feel safe and happy. What about your current environment makes you feel safe (or unsafe)? What makes you feel happy or unhappy? Then, write about your ideal environment.

Today, I will practice self-care by _____

Mood Tracker 😄 🙂 😐 😮 😟 🙁 ☹️ 😣

Drinking enough water is one of the easiest ways to ensure we're giving our bodies what they need. But we often don't have a good idea of how much water we're actually drinking. Today, every time you take a drink of water, record it here. How much water did you drink today?

_____

_____

_____

_____

_____

_____

_____

_____

_____

_____

_____

_____

_____

Today, I will practice self-care by _____

Mood Tracker   😃 🙂 😐 😮 🙁 😕 ☹️ 😣

Sometimes it can be difficult to appreciate every part of your body when you're focused on your outer appearance. Regardless of what you look like, your body is capable of some pretty amazing things. What part of your body do you appreciate right now? What did it do for you today?

_____

_____

_____

_____

_____

_____

_____

_____

_____

_____

_____

_____

_____

_____

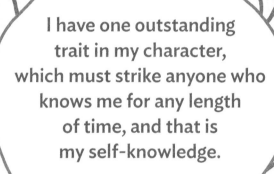

I have one outstanding trait in my character, which must strike anyone who knows me for any length of time, and that is my self-knowledge.

—ANNE FRANK

Charging the Heart

How we view ourselves can tremendously affect our lives. It is important to cultivate and develop self-awareness and self-love. When we do, we can go into the world and show up as our best selves.

Being our best selves not only helps us but also helps our friends and family. Cultivating self-love can help us be better friends, better communicators, and better human beings.

Admittedly, self-love isn't something that comes easily. However, the fact that you're reading this page shows that there's already a spark of self-love in you.

Today, I will practice self-care by _____

_____

Mood Tracker 😀 🙂 😐 😮 😟 😕 😔 ☹️

Self-love, like a lot of things, makes more sense when you define it. So, what is self-love to you? If you loved yourself, what things would you do? How would you feel? What would you not be afraid of?

_____

_____

_____

_____

_____

_____

_____

_____

_____

_____

_____

_____

_____

_____

_____

_____

Today, I will practice self-care by _____

Mood Tracker 😃 🙂 😐 😮 😥 🙁 😖 😣

We all need help sometimes. But asking for help can be difficult and takes courage. In what ways have you seen others ask for help? How did it make you feel when they reached out?

_____

_____

_____

_____

_____

_____

_____

_____

_____

_____

_____

_____

_____

_____

_____

_____

Today, I will practice self-care by _____

Mood Tracker 😀 🙂 😐 😮 😢 😕 😟 ☹️

Holding on to grudges or negative thoughts about others can have a significant effect on our mental health. They take up our time, energy, and emotional capacity. Are you currently holding a grudge or having negative thoughts about someone? What happened? Why are you holding on to it? How can you move past it?

_____

_____

_____

_____

_____

_____

_____

_____

_____

_____

_____

_____

_____

_____

Today, I will practice self-care by _____

Mood Tracker   😄 🙂 😐 😮 😣 🙁 ☹️ 😞

Loss is a part of life, and losing people is sadly something everyone will go through. Losing someone doesn't always mean that they have died. Loss can happen when someone moves away or spends less time with us. Missing someone because of a loss is expected. Is there anyone that you're missing right now? What do you miss about them?

_____

_____

_____

_____

_____

_____

_____

_____

_____

_____

_____

_____

_____

Today, I will practice self-care by

Mood Tracker

Everyone makes mistakes. You may even make the same mistakes more than once. That's okay. What's more important is that you learn something from mistakes. Think about a mistake that you made, and write down what you learned from it.

For this exercise, spend some time looking in the mirror. The size of the mirror doesn't matter. Take a good look at yourself and smile. Continue to look at yourself and give yourself at least five compliments. These compliments can be about anything: your appearance, your personality, your relationships with others, etc. I know this may feel uncomfortable at first, but saying kind things to yourself is often uncomfortable. We give praise easily to others but often fail to praise ourselves. This short exercise can go a long way toward changing that.

Today, I will practice self-care by _____

Mood Tracker   😄 🙂 😐 😮 😖 🙁 😔 ☹️

Some of our innermost thoughts are about things we're afraid of. Usually, the more we understand something, the less we are scared of it. Knowledge truly is powerful. What are some things you're fearful of, and how can you learn more about these fears?

_____

_____

_____

_____

_____

_____

_____

_____

_____

_____

_____

_____

_____

_____

_____

_____

Today, I will practice self-care by

Mood Tracker

Helping people can be a fantastic way to show our inner selves to the outside world. Supporting and helping others can look different depending on who you are. How can you be supportive of other people in your own unique way?

Water is a good metaphor for getting rid of things we don't want. We wash away things like germs and dirt because they can make us sick. The next time you're in the shower or bath, or even the next time you wash your hands, think about all of the negative things you want to wash away. All of the negative thoughts. All of the worries. Visualize them all going down the drain.

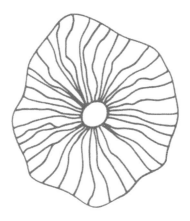

Today, I will practice self-care by _____

| *Mood Tracker* | 😃 | 🙂 | 😐 | 😲 | 😢 | 😟 | 😞 | 😣 |

There are people in our lives we feel closer to than other people. They may be friends, siblings, parents, or grandparents. Often, we are close to these people because of how they make us feel when we're with them. Who do you feel close to? What makes them someone you want to be close to?

_____

_____

_____

_____

_____

_____

_____

_____

_____

_____

_____

_____

_____

_____

_____

Today, I will practice self-care by _____

Mood Tracker   😄 🙂 😐 😲 😖 😕 🙁 😣

Is honesty the best policy? Many people will tell you that we lie to ourselves just as often as (or even more often than) we do to others. Do you think you're lying to yourself about anything? How can you be more honest with yourself?

The best and
most beautiful things
in the world cannot
be seen nor even touched,
but just felt in the heart.

—HELEN KELLER

Today, I will practice self-care by _____

| _Mood Tracker_ | 😄 😊 😐 😮 😢 😞 😔 ☹️ |

We all have negative thoughts about ourselves sometimes. This is entirely normal and nothing to be ashamed of. Write down some of the negative thoughts that you have about yourself on one side of the line. Replace those thoughts with positive ones on the other. Here's an example. Negative thought: I'm dumb for caring about people. Positive thought: Caring about people makes me compassionate.

NEGATIVE THOUGHT → POSITIVE THOUGHT

Today, I will practice self-care by _____

Mood Tracker	😄 😊 😐 😯 😢 😕 🙁 ☹️

Self-love looks and feels different for everyone. In this current moment right now, do you love yourself? Why or why not? What do you feel would help you get to a place where you love yourself?

_____

_____

_____

_____

_____

_____

_____

_____

_____

_____

_____

_____

_____

Today, I will practice self-care by _____

Mood Tracker   😄 🙂 😐 😮 😟 🙁 ☹️ 😣

It is normal to feel a wide range of emotions from day to day, but sometimes people get stuck in only a few emotions. This may not be an issue if your prevailing emotion is happiness, but if it is sadness or anger, it can lead to negative self-esteem. Think about your emotions today and write them down here. What did you notice?

Today, I will practice self-care by

| *Mood Tracker* | 😀 | 🙂 | 😐 | 😯 | 😢 | 😕 | 😟 | 😣 |

You know yourself best. There are things you love and skills you have that you probably haven't shared with anyone else. How awesome is it to have hidden skills? What's your secret passion or hidden talent? How can you use this as a form of self-care?

Today, I will practice self-care by _____

Mood Tracker 😀 🙂 😐 😮 😢 😟 😫 😖

Sometimes when we have low self-esteem, we apologize more often than we should. We might apologize for crying when we're feeling hurt or for needing support. Figuring out what to say instead of apologizing in the moment can be difficult, so let's come up with some things you can say now. For situations in which you feel like you might apologize for just being you, write down some other ways you can respond.

Today, I will practice self-care by _____

Mood Tracker

Every person has instincts or little voices inside their head that tell them to do or not do things. Sometimes it can be hard to trust these instincts, but they usually won't lead you wrong. Do you trust your instincts? Why or why not?

Have you ever been rummaging through your closet and found a note you or someone else wrote that made you smile? Why not make yourself smile with notes from yourself? All you need for this exercise is a pen and paper. Write down compliments or words of encouragement. Hide them all over your house or room. You'll eventually forget about them, and it will be a wonderful surprise to find them when you least expect it.

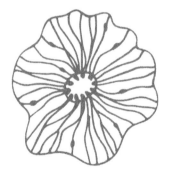

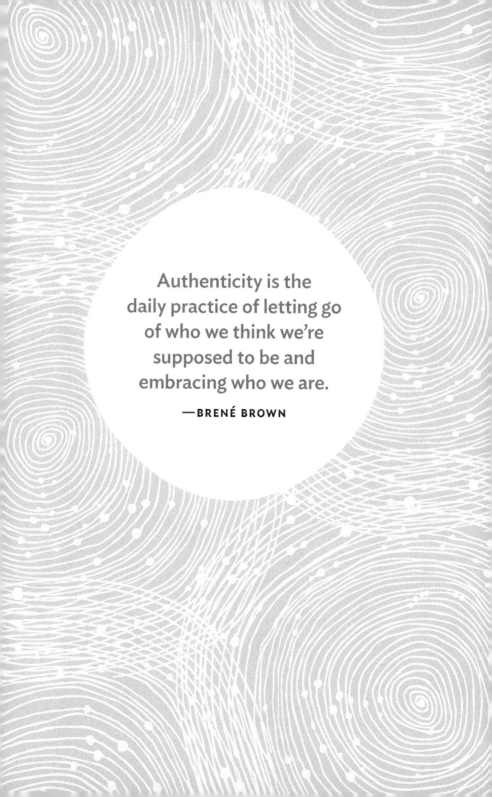

Authenticity is the daily practice of letting go of who we think we're supposed to be and embracing who we are.

—BRENÉ BROWN

Today, I will practice self-care by _____

Mood Tracker 😄 🙂 😐 😮 😧 😕 🙁 ☹️

Positive affirmations are a great way to start building up your self-esteem. There are many ways you can write positive affirmations. One of the most popular is the "I Am" statement. Here's an example: "I am a good person." Write down five positive affirmations using "I Am" statements (or any other style you like).

_____

_____

_____

_____

_____

_____

_____

_____

_____

_____

_____

_____

_____

Today, I will practice self-care by _____

Mood Tracker 😄 🙂 😐 😯 😢 🙁 😞 😖

Everyone gets heartbroken from time to time. Heartbreak does not have to come from the loss of a romantic relationship. It can come from anywhere and from any type of love. How do you repair a broken heart? Write down your cure.

Today, I will practice self-care by _____

Mood Tracker   😀   🙂   😐   😮   😢   🙁   😣   ☹️

Our friends and family members know a lot about us. Sometimes they even see qualities in us that we're unable to see in ourselves. How do you think your closest friend or family member would describe you? (Feel free to ask them if that makes this easier.)

Today, I will practice self-care by

A simple way to get all of your feelings and thoughts out is by writing a letter to yourself. Use this space to do just that. Your letter to yourself can be as long or as short as you want. Detail your disappointments, your triumphs, your hopes, your dreams, and anything else that you'd like.

One of the easiest (and best!) ways to outwardly express self-love is by doing something for someone else. You may have heard of "paying it forward" or performing random acts of kindness. For this exercise, that's exactly what you'll do. You do not have to spend money to perform a random act of kindness. Anything kind that you do for someone else counts. Here are a few ideas:

Shovel snow or rake leaves for a neighbor

Tell someone that they have a nice smile

Donate something you don't need to a charity

Cook a meal for a family member

To be beautiful
means to be yourself.
You don't need to be accepted
by others. You need to
accept yourself.

—THICH NHAT HANH

Today, I will practice self-care by _____

Mood Tracker 😀 🙂 😐 😮 😣 🙁 😔 😞

Sometimes our self-esteem suffers because we've forgotten all of the great things we've achieved. Think of when you did something you never thought you could, like getting a good grade on an exam or landing your first job. Really immerse yourself in that moment. What feelings did you have? What small accomplishments made it possible? How can you carry that sense of pride forward?

Today, I will practice self-care by _____

| *Mood Tracker* | 😄 | 🙂 | 😐 | 😯 | 😣 | 🙁 | ☹️ | 😕 |

Losing something doesn't always have to be a negative experience. It can also be rewarding. For example, you can lose your fear of asking for help. What are some things you have lost that were positive? What made losing them positive?

_____

_____

_____

_____

_____

_____

_____

_____

_____

_____

_____

_____

_____

_____

_____

_____

Asking for help is one of the hardest things that we ever have to do as humans. Too often, we let our pride or shame get in the way of telling someone we need their support. Asking for help is okay. Think of something that you need help with. It can be something small, like needing someone to dry the dishes after you wash them, or more significant, like talking about difficult or complicated emotions. After you figure out what you need help with, ask someone to help you. The more you ask for help, the easier it gets.

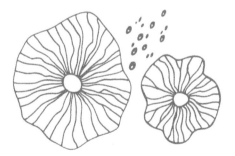

Today, I will practice self-care by _____

Mood Tracker	☺ ☺ ☺ ☺ ☺ ☺ ☺ ☺

Creating boundaries is a challenging but effective way to protect ourselves and our well-being. You can set boundaries for activities, people, experiences, etc. An example of a boundary is telling a friend you don't want to talk about your family life. What boundaries do you currently have in place? In what areas (or with which people) do you need better boundaries?

_____

_____

_____

_____

_____

_____

_____

_____

_____

_____

_____

_____

_____

_____

Today, I will practice self-care by _____

Mood Tracker   😃 🙂 😐 😮 😟 😦 😧 😣

One way we can understand ourselves is by knowing how we interact with and love other people. How do you show love for others? Do you think you love different people in different ways?

_____

_____

_____

_____

_____

_____

_____

_____

_____

_____

_____

_____

_____

_____

_____

Today, I will practice self-care by _____

Mood Tracker   😁   🙂   😐   😮   😢   🙁   ☹️   😣

We've talked about the self-love benefits of writing a letter to yourself as you are right now, but writing a letter to your future self can also create a sense of self-love. In this letter, talk about all of the fantastic things you're going to do for yourself right now so that your future self is happy and cared for.

_____

_____

_____

_____

_____

_____

_____

_____

_____

_____

_____

_____

_____

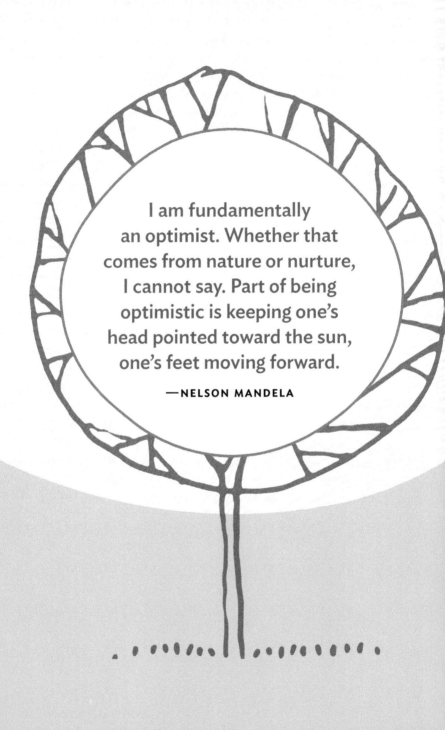

I am fundamentally
an optimist. Whether that
comes from nature or nurture,
I cannot say. Part of being
optimistic is keeping one's
head pointed toward the sun,
one's feet moving forward.

—NELSON MANDELA

Nurturing the Mind & Spirit

Nurturing your mind and spirit is an integral part of self-care. When you nourish your mind and soul, you'll find it easier to get through the everyday stresses of life.

Caring for these two parts of your being builds upon the foundation of self-care that you laid when you first opened this book.

The more in tune you are with yourself and the world around you, the better equipped you'll be to move forward and grow. You'll find a life for yourself that allows you to flourish and thrive.

Today, I will practice self-care by _____

Mood Tracker   😄   🙂   😐   😮   😰   🙁   😦   😧

Your life is probably packed with things you have to do and places you need to be. Even with all of the hustle and bustle of our lives, there are moments of silence and peace. What made a moment today peaceful?

_____

_____

_____

_____

_____

_____

_____

_____

_____

_____

_____

_____

Today, I will practice self-care by _____

Mood Tracker   😃 🙂 😐 😲 😟 🙁 😞 😣

We've all gone through challenges, whether big or small, that test our strength and resilience. When you're experiencing a challenge, what helps get you through it? How can you make sure you use these coping skills in the future?

_____

_____

_____

_____

_____

_____

_____

_____

_____

_____

_____

_____

_____

_____

_____

_____

Today, I will practice self-care by _____

Mood Tracker 😄 🙂 😐 😮 😢 😕 😟 ☹️

The concept of having a growth mindset instead of a fixed mindset has become increasingly popular. A fixed mindset assumes things are set in stone and can't be changed, while a growth mindset assumes that things are fluid and change is possible. Do you think you have a fixed mindset or a growth mindset? Why?

One way to deeply connect with yourself is through mindfulness and meditation. A fun and easy way to practice mindfulness is taking a mindful walk. Don't bring anything with you besides the necessities, like your phone and keys. Don't bring headphones, so you're not tempted to listen to music or watch videos. While you're on your walk, notice what it feels like when your feet hit the ground. Notice how the air feels around you. Notice what thoughts come up for you now that you don't have the distractions of the everyday.

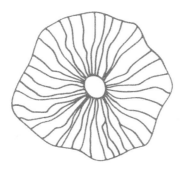

Today, I will practice self-care by _____

Mood Tracker 😄 😊 😐 😮 😟 😕 🙁 😣

Key to the foundation of who we are (and who we can grow to be) are our values and morals. Your values are the things that you believe are important (like honesty or responsibility). Your morals define what you think is acceptable and unacceptable. Morals and values often go hand in hand. What do you value, and what are your morals? How do they work together? How do they differ?

Today, I will practice self-care by _____

Mood Tracker 😄 🙂 😐 😮 😟 😕 🙁 😣

We all have things that make us happy. But some things make us happier than others. Think about all of the things that make you happy. When are you happiest? How can you incorporate more happiness into your life?

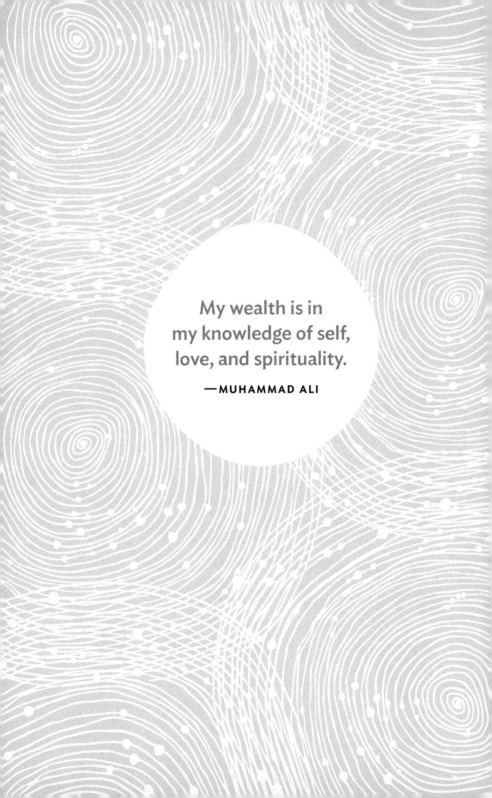

My wealth is in
my knowledge of self,
love, and spirituality.

—MUHAMMAD ALI

Today, I will practice self-care by

Mood Tracker

Learning from our experiences, even the seemingly uneventful ones, can lead to opportunities for growth. Today, write down five things that you learned from some of these more subtle experiences. They don't have to be serious, life-changing, or particularly thoughtful (but they can be!).

Today, I will practice self-care by _____

| Mood Tracker | 😄 | 🙂 | 😐 | 😮 | 😟 | 😕 | 😔 | ☹️ |

As you get older, you can start to equate your purpose in life with your job. In reality, your career isn't always your whole purpose, but it can influence many things in your life. So, let's think about it. What's your ideal job or career path?

_____

_____

_____

_____

_____

_____

_____

_____

_____

_____

_____

_____

_____

_____

_____

_____

Today, I will practice self-care by _____

Mood Tracker   😄 🙂 😐 😯 🙁 😕 ☹️ 😣

Sometimes, what spurs our growth is the desire to have the same
qualities as someone we admire. There is a lot that we can learn from
other people. Who do you admire most? What about them do you
admire? What opportunities can you look for to gain some of the
qualities they have?

_____

_____

_____

_____

_____

_____

_____

_____

_____

_____

_____

_____

_____

Learning from situations in which we grow is one of the best ways to move forward with our lives. However, seeking out growth opportunities, or even saying yes to them when they are presented to us, can be difficult. Why? Because growth requires us to step out of our comfort zones. Today, be mindful of opportunities to get out of your comfort zone. This might mean signing up for a class on a subject you haven't studied before or walking up to someone and starting a conversation. Lean into being uncomfortable for a little while. Even if it is hard at first, I guarantee it will get easier the more you do it.

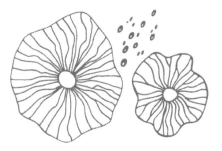

Today, I will practice self-care by _____

Mood Tracker 😄 🙂 😐 😮 😢 😕 ☹️ 🙁

Joy can be found in the tiniest of ordinary moments, like finding a snack buried deep in a cabinet or getting a compliment from a stranger. Everyone finds joy in different places and experiences. Where do you find joy?

Today, I will practice self-care by _____

Mood Tracker   ☺ ☺ 😐 😯 😢 ☹ ☹ ☹

Our parents, grandparents, and other family members have a strong influence on us, especially when we're growing up. How have your parents or other family members influenced your spiritual beliefs and beliefs about yourself? Was this influence positive or negative, or perhaps even harmful? (Sometimes talking about our families can be triggering. If you're feeling triggered, you can practice a self-care technique like grounding [see page 2] or reach out to a crisis intervention service [see Resources, page 141].)

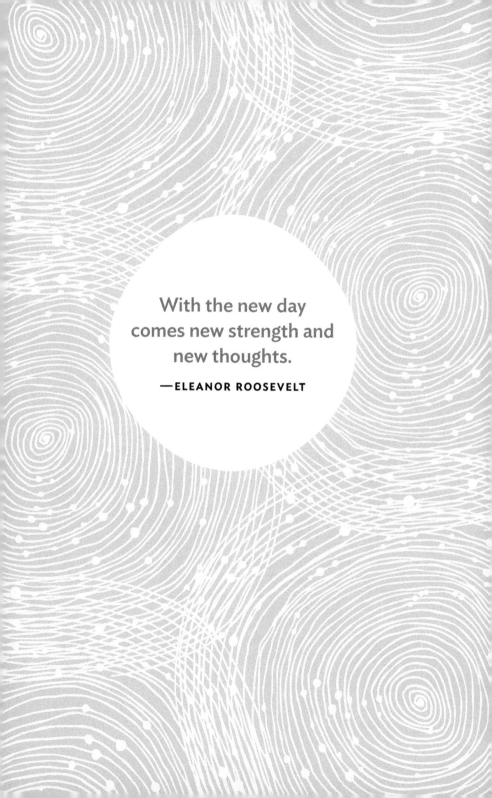

With the new day
comes new strength and
new thoughts.

—ELEANOR ROOSEVELT

Today, I will practice self-care by _____

Mood Tracker 😄 🙂 😐 😮 😢 😕 😟 ☹️

Many people have had experiences that lead them to believe in a universal connection. Talk about an experience where you felt especially connected to the universe or humanity as a whole.

_____

_____

_____

_____

_____

_____

_____

_____

_____

_____

_____

_____

_____

_____

_____

Today, I will practice self-care by _____

Mood Tracker 😀 🙂 😐 😮 😢 🙁 ☹️ 😞

Thinking about your future can be pretty exciting. Tomorrow holds many possibilities. What excites you about your future? If nothing feels exciting right now, that's okay. You can even write about what excites you about the future in general. (Maybe flying cars?!)

Creativity can be a great way to connect to your inner self and express that self outwardly. There are many ways you can be creative, from writing and drawing to photography and making videos. You probably have many things around your house that can help you start a creative project: pens, scissors, old magazines, glue, and even your phone or laptop. Take some time today to figure out a creative project that you can undertake. Then gather your materials and actually do it! Don't be afraid to think outside the box.

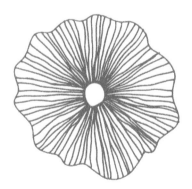

Today, I will practice self-care by _____

Mood Tracker 😃 🙂 😐 😮 😟 😕 🙁 😣

We don't only get our beliefs from family and friends; we get them from influencers, celebrities, authors, musicians, and athletes, too. How have these types of people influenced your beliefs? Are these influences different from those of your family and friends?

_____

_____

_____

_____

_____

_____

_____

_____

_____

_____

_____

_____

_____

_____

_____

_____

_____

Today, I will practice self-care by _____

Mood Tracker   😀 🙂 😐 😮 😢 🙁 ☹️ 😣

One of the easiest ways to find joy is by incorporating things that make us happy into our days. Give some thought about how you can make tomorrow joyful, and write down what you're going to do. For example, you can schedule time to meet with a friend or watch a favorite movie.

Today, I will practice self-care by _____

Mood Tracker 😄 🙂 😐 😮 😢 🙁 ☹️ 😞

When we grow and change, sometimes we need to leave specific ideas, places, habits, or even people behind. It's not rude to move forward in your life without these things if they don't enhance your growth. What might you have to leave behind to move forward and continue to grow?

_____

_____

_____

_____

_____

_____

_____

_____

_____

_____

_____

_____

_____

Decide what you want. Declare it to the world. See yourself winning. And remember that if you are persistent as well as patient, you can get whatever you seek.

—MISTY COPELAND

Today, I will practice self-care by

Mood Tracker 😄 🙂 😐 😮 😟 🙁 😣 😞

Just as self-care is different for everyone, spirituality is different for everyone, too. Spirituality is not just religion (or the absence of religion); it can also include things like your morals or your thoughts about your greater impact on the world. How would you describe your spirituality?

Today, I will practice self-care by _____

Mood Tracker   😀 🙂 😐 😮 😖 😟 😔 ☹️

After experiencing a growth opportunity, it can help to go back and think about how else you could have approached the situation. Over the past couple of days, you've probably had some growth opportunities. Think back on one of them, and write about what you could have done better.

_____

_____

_____

_____

_____

_____

_____

_____

_____

_____

_____

_____

_____

In a prompt on page 101, we explored the process of understanding and creating boundaries. Boundaries can protect not only our emotional well-being but also our minds and spirits. Often, you might do things just because you feel like you should, even though they conflict with your spirit, that innermost part of you that encompasses everything you are. The next time that you encounter an opportunity to practice setting a boundary, do it.

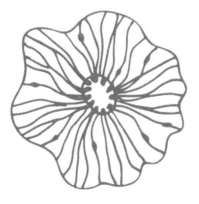

Today, I will practice self-care by _____

We are all unique and have different talents and gifts. You may think that your gift (like having a beautiful singing voice) is not unique. But, because everyone is different, no one has your exact gift. What are your gifts, or what are you good at? How can you impact others with your skills?

Today, I will practice self-care by _____

_____

Mood Tracker   😄 🙂 😐 😮 😢 🙁 ☹️ 😣

You may have had at least one experience in your life when you felt spiritually connected to what was happening around you. More than likely, you've had multiple. What has been your most significant spiritual experience? Remember, spiritual experiences don't have to involve religion. They can also involve a connection to nature, other people, or the universe at large.

_____

_____

_____

_____

_____

_____

_____

_____

_____

_____

_____

_____

_____

Today, I will practice self-care by _____

In school, from your parents, on television, and elsewhere, you may have heard a lot about "finding your purpose." That sounds like an enormous task to embark on right now, so let's start smaller. What's your life's purpose for just this month?

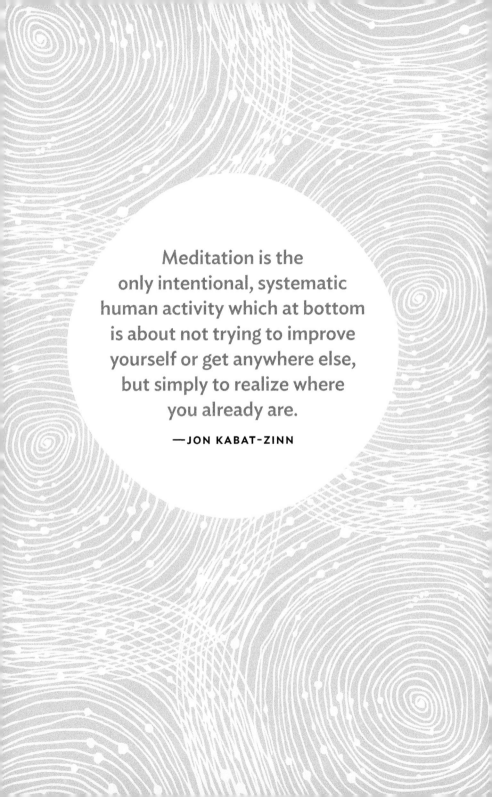

Meditation is the
only intentional, systematic
human activity which at bottom
is about not trying to improve
yourself or get anywhere else,
but simply to realize where
you already are.

—JON KABAT-ZINN

Today, I will practice self-care by _____

Mood Tracker   😄 🙂 😐 😮 😣 😕 😟 ☹️

Being creative can be one of the best ways to express your inner worldview. When was the last time you were creative? What did you do? How can you bring that creativity back?

Today, I will practice self-care by _____

Mood Tracker   😄   🙂   😐   😮   😟   😕   😣   ☹️

There are probably spiritual practices that you've heard of and want to know more about, like mindfulness or meditation. What spiritual practices are you curious about? How can you find out more about them?

_____

_____

_____

_____

_____

_____

_____

_____

_____

_____

_____

_____

_____

_____

Today, I will practice self-care by _____

Cultivating a mindset that welcomes growth and change, particularly if you're starting out with a fixed mindset, can be difficult. But it is possible! Affirmations targeted specifically at growth and change can help. Write down at least five positive affirmations that you can use when you need to shift into a growth mindset. Here's one example: "I will learn something new from every experience."

Breathing, and especially breathing deeply, can bring a few moments of calm in an otherwise hectic day. Many of us breathe shallowly. "Belly breathing" or "diaphragmatic breathing" can alleviate stress and help you feel more relaxed. Follow the steps below to practice belly breathing:

Get into a comfortable position

Begin to breathe as you normally do

Focus on inhaling through your nose and exhaling through your mouth (this may be different from how you normally breathe)

Place a hand on your stomach to gauge the depth of your breathing (your belly should be expanding with your breath)

Continue to breathe in this way until you feel a sense of calm

Today, I will practice self-care by _____

Changing our habits and behaviors can help us build up the strength to change our lives. What habits or behaviors do you think are inhibiting you from living your life to the fullest? What can you do to change them?

Today, I will practice self-care by _____

Mood Tracker   😄 🙂 😐 😮 😢 🙁 ☹️ 😖

Today, let's dream big! Knowing and expressing our biggest hopes and dreams can lead us to seek opportunities that will make them come true. What are you hoping for and dreaming of in your life? Nothing is too big or too small. What's one step you can take now that will help you move toward getting there?

Resources

Blessing Manifesting: BlessingManifesting.com
Blessing Manifesting is a self-care and self-love website perfect for people just beginning their self-care journeys.

The Gifts of Imperfection by Brené Brown
The Gifts of Imperfection is an inspirational book on how to be authentically yourself and cultivate feelings of self-worth.

Learning to Be Free: LearningToBeFree.com
Learning to Be Free is a one-stop shop for everything you need to grow as an individual, straight from the author of this book.

Practicing Mindfulness by Matthew Sockolov
In *Practicing Mindfulness*, you'll learn to implement mindfulness and meditation practices to keep calm in your day-to-day life.

A Year of Positive Thinking by Cyndie Spiegel
A Year of Positive Thinking pushes you to find the positive in every day of the year with prompts, exercises, and reflections.

Crisis Intervention Services

Crisis Text Line: CrisisTextLine.org, or text HOME to 741741 in the United States and Canada, 85258 in the United Kingdom, or 50808 in Ireland
Crisis Text Line provides free, 24/7, confidential crisis intervention services via text message or Facebook Messenger.

National Suicide Prevention Lifeline: SuicidePreventionLifeline.org, or (1-800) 273-8255
The National Suicide Prevention Lifeline provides free, 24/7, confidential crisis intervention services across the United States via phone or online chat.

About the Author

 Briana Hollis is a licensed social worker, life coach, and higher education professional who has worked with hundreds of clients and students, helping them figure out how to live their best lives with mental health, career, and education support.

Briana holds a Master of Science in Social Administration from Case Western Reserve University and a Master of Education in Higher Education Administration from Tiffin University.

In her free time, she loves to read, spend time with her family, and play with her cat, Chloe.

She blogs about self-care, self-discovery, and self-improvement at Learning to Be Free (LearningToBeFree.com).

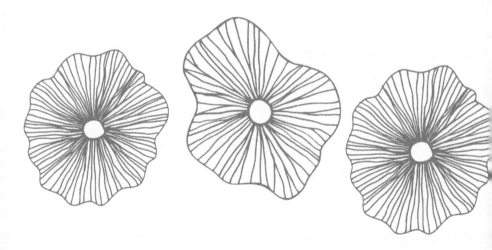